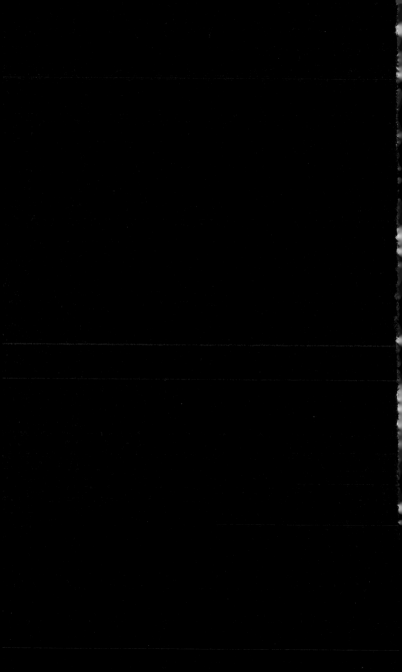

LURCHING TOWARD HAPPINESS IN AMERICA

LURCHING TOWARD HAPPINESS IN AMERICA

Claude S. Fischer

A Boston Review Book

THE MIT PRESS   Cambridge, Mass.   London, England

MIT Press books may be purchased at special quantity discounts for business or sales promotional use. For information, please email special_sales@mitpress.mit.edu.

This book was set in Adobe Garamond by *Boston Review* and was printed and bound in the United States of America.

Library of Congress Cataloging-in-Publication Data

Fischer, Claude S., 1948–
Lurching toward happiness in America / Claude Fischer.
    pages   cm. — (Boston review books)
ISBN 978-0-262-02824-0 (hardcover : alk. paper)
1. Quality of life—United States. 2. Happiness—United States. 3. United States—Civilization—21st century. 4. United States—Social conditions—21st century. 5. United States—Economic conditions—21st century. I. Title.
HN60.F566   2014
306—dc23
                                                    2014031350

10 9 8 7 6 5 4 3 2 1

In memory of Ralph Fischer

CONTENTS

INTRODUCTION

WHAT ARE WE TO MAKE OF THE STRIKING second sentence of the Declaration of Independence—that the new nation would be dedicated to defending not only a citizen's life and liberty, but also "the pursuit of happiness"? The phrase replaced "property" in the trio of "unalienable rights" that had been circulating among insurrectionists in the colonies. Whatever the thinking that led to that change, it exemplified the egalitarianism of the nation-in-process: each person, propertied or not, ought to be sufficiently unencumbered to run after his own happiness, whatever doing so entailed. "Person," of course, was implicitly qualified to exclude slaves and women, but the egalitarian creed had been endorsed—even if it took centuries to become more fully universal.

Empowering a citizenry to pursue happiness requires more than merely sustaining life and safeguarding liberty. It requires, for one thing, a base of financial security. The success of the social egalitarian experiment in America has always hinged to a great extent on the promise of economic success. Helped immeasurably by the bountifulness of the land and the energy of immigrants, early America became a dynamic economic engine. By the mid-twentieth century, most Americans were secure enough to run after happiness; it was a democratically shared pursuit. That a few groups were still excluded was a blatant embarrassment.

In recent decades, though, many Americans' economic security has been shaken: chasing after happiness increasingly looks like a luxury, not an unalienable right. The strides we take to happiness seem more and more like isolated lurches than steady gains. The gap between the poor and the rich, and even between the insecurely and the securely wealthy, has grown, undermining the universalism of the American Dream. As our country emerges from the Great Recession, we can only speculate whether the recent past will signal a permanent retreat from the long course of American history, or only a temporary detour.

This book addresses anxieties about the pursuit of happiness in America today. What exactly is happiness? How can we measure it? And what role should our government and our communities play in helping people pursue it? Our anxieties about these questions concern not only growing economic insecurity and inequality, but also other changes in the fabric of our cultural and social lives, such as the Internet revolution, gender relations, and divisive politics. By putting these issues into sociological and historical context, I try to illuminate where we have come from and where we are going.

Part I

Plumbing Unhappiness

1. Happiness Policy

WHAT DO WE KNOW ABOUT HAPPINESS?

Since at least the 1950s, academics have analyzed surveys asking people how happy or satisfied they feel. To assess morale we've used fuzzy questions such as, "Taken all together, how would you say things are these days—would you say that you are very happy, pretty happy, or not too happy?" We've compared, say, women to men and the poor to the rich. Dutch sociologist Ruut Veenhoven started compiling the findings into his *World Database of Happiness* back in the 1980s.

We know so far that people's reports of immediate joy and misery fluctuate from activity to activity—sex is an upper; commuting is a downer—and often diverge notably from the summary answers they give to questions about their happiness "these days." We also know that subjective well-being can be complex. People can be happy about work and sad about love; the latter usually matters more. The opposite of happiness, research suggests, is not necessarily despair, but apathy; some people just don't feel much of anything.

Nonetheless, people who say they are generally happy tend to be economically secure, married, healthy, religious, and busy with friends; they tend to live in affluent, democratic, individualistic societies with activist, welfare-state governments. The connection between reporting happiness and personal traits often runs both ways. For example, being healthy adds to happiness, and happy people also stay healthier.

Researchers have been especially interested in whether money makes people happy. We know that being poor makes people less happy. Some researchers argue, however, that having more money beyond that needed for basic security returns no additional happiness and can even create unhappiness. Making more money may be fruitless because people adapt psychologically to their levels of wealth and, like addicts and drugs, need ever more money to get the same level of pleasure. Or perhaps it's not really about the money; it's about position. People chase money to feel superior to the folks next door. That, of course, becomes a vicious and pointless cycle. Other researchers, including Veenhoven, agree that the more money one makes, the more money it takes to move the happiness meter, but they nevertheless insist that more money—unlike the futile experience with drugs—does bring more happiness, albeit at a slower pace among the well-to-do. The data appear to support that position.

The money-happiness question was initially raised in the 1970s by economist Richard Easterlin, who observed that growing affluence since the mid-twentieth century had not led to more reports of happiness in national surveys. (Actually, Freud raised a similar question in *Civilization and Its Discontents*, in 1929.) One explanation of the Easterlin Paradox, aside from adaptation and competition, is that increasing materialism ruined the pleasure Americans might have gotten from becoming wealthier. Some, including myself, have argued that there is no paradox to start with, because the growing wealth since the 1970s has concentrated in the hands of the few. Average Americans haven't gotten happier in part because average Americans haven't really gotten wealthier.

In recent years there has been a renewed stampede to study happiness, and, especially, to create happiness measures for national policy. Bhutan's Gross National Happiness Commission uses citizens' reports of their happiness to assess national progress. Former French President Nicholas Sarkozy appointed a Nobel-encrusted commission to study a similar idea. The United Nations places "happiness indicators" on its war-burdened agenda; American science institutions pour money into fine-tuning measurements of "subjective well-being"; and Amazon's list of happiness books by moonlighting professors runs from *The Happiness Hypothesis* to *Stumbling on Happiness*, *Authentic Happiness*, *Engineering Happiness*, and beyond.

What set off this frenzy? Economists found happiness.

In the decade after 2000, the number of articles on happiness in major economics journals roughly tripled. One economist told me a few years ago that his colleagues' pursuit of happiness was depressing him. Nonetheless, established leaders and bright new scholars turned to the topic and brought with them the funding, media prestige, and political clout of the profession. That a guild which prides itself on scientific rigor and hardheadedness would embrace such a sappy concept measured in such mushy ways is, well, bemusing. Even former Federal Reserve Chief Ben Bernanke drew on the new economics of happiness to find the moral for his 2010 commencement address to University of South Carolina graduates: "I urge you to take this research to heart by making time for friends and family and by being part of and contributing to a larger community."

The embrace resulted, I think, from the great challenge the emergence of behavioral economics posed to the discipline. Standard economics assumes that people are rational deciders, and they reveal their preferences, what gives them "utility," by their choices. But people often have confused preferences, make sub-optimal selections, and regret their decisions. Because of this, Nobel Prize–winner Daniel Kahneman and former Chair of the Council of Economic Advisers Alan Krueger wrote in 2006, "An exclusive reliance on choices to infer what people desire loses some of its appeal."

If economics is all about individuals optimizing their utility, but that utility is not revealed by people's actual choices, how then do we know which economic behaviors and policies are optimal? Track happiness. Kahneman and Kreuger have mounted projects to do just that, trying to bring the measurement precision of, say, steel production reports and the Fed's overnight interest rate to happiness. Study subjects are asked to list their activities of the previous day and rate the pleasure and pain they felt then. (This is cheaper than "experience sampling," in which subjects report their moment-by-moment feelings via a pager or similar device.) The returns from this research investment have so far been slight.

The experts pressing for happiness indicators are reacting to policymakers' habit of assessing progress only in terms such as the Gross National Product. Happiness researchers propose blending their numbers with other measures of well-being, such as health statistics, educational attainment, social ties, political voice, and sustainability. Theirs is a generous and democratic impulse.

Still, cautions are in order. Politically, this move expands the generation-long division between tree-hugger and lunch-bucket liberals. "Post-materialists," who believe that Americans have wrung out all the happiness wealth can surrender, argue that we should work on other sources of happiness, such as personal relationships and experiencing nature. Materialists, who believe that too many Americans are stuck way below some wealth-and-happiness optimum, argue that we should keep pushing for more and better-paid jobs. It's sort of Seattle Democrats versus Youngstown Democrats.

But, more broadly, we must ask if happiness is always the bottom line—the metric by which all events in our lives are to be evaluated. Should we discount tragedies because research shows that victims typically recover their happiness? Should happiness data decide policy? (Where economists are involved, policy is rarely far away.) Could a drug such as *Brave New World*'s soma, or an app that stimulates the brain's pleasure centers, be the ultimate policy tool? Talk about happiness today leaves questions such as these unanswered.

In 2012 the happily contrarian economist Deirdre McCloskey unleashed a cannonade on happiness research in *The New Republic*. She points out that the happiness industry brings us back to Benthamite aspirations to assess utility as if by the tailor's yardstick. She dismisses the measurement technology and, more fundamentally, the emphasis on happiness over material conditions. That concern emerges, she sneers, from the snooty literati's contempt, born of romantic pastoralism, for the material needs of average folks. She asks what gives us most meaning in life and—ending up sounding pretty Seattle-ish herself—suggests it is more often found in painful striving than in achievement.

Whatever the philosophical issues around happiness—yes, the philosophy professors have also joined the pursuit—asking people questions about their feelings of well-being is a useful diagnostic tool for research. We learn, for instance, that increasing economic inequality since the 1970s widened the class gap in feelings of happiness and that the job and income losses of the Great Recession have depressed Americans' average happiness. But these are rough measures, and whether they can or should guide national policy remains an open question. Even as these abstract speculations abound, around us the material world is changing, typically unguided by conscious policy. Americans are making their way through these new landscapes, such as the online world, in seeking the good life.

2. E-Disharmony?

OVER THE LAST FEW YEARS *The Atlantic* HAS found a rich source of click bait by featuring arguments that the Internet is destroying the good life. In 2008 Google was making us stupid; in 2012 Facebook was making us lonely; and in 2013 online dating was "threatening monogamy."

The latest argument is that e-dating makes it so easy for people to meet romantic partners that it undermines their commitments to any one person. The central proof author Dan Slater provides is the extended tale of one "Jacob," a man who fires up his dating sites while his latest girlfriend is walking out the door. His major life chore is scheduling his hook-ups. Presumably, before e-dating Jacob would have reconciled himself to a minimally satisfying long-term marriage. Instead, his Don Juan life shows that "the rise of online dating will mean an overall decrease in commitment."

Now, when it comes to making and breaking commitments, there is some actual evidence one easily could turn to, though Slater doesn't. Match.com went online in 1995, Yahoo! Personals in 1998, e-Harmony in 2000. By 2000, American couples were as likely to have met online as in college. In other words, e-dating was immediately popular.

So what happened to marriage and divorce rates in the age of online dating?

For the past fifty years, Americans have been marrying later and later. But as e-dating has grown, the trend to postpone marrying has actually slowed down. In 1980 the average American woman married for the first time at the age of 22. Between 1980 and 1990, the average rose 1.9 years; between 1990 and 2000 it rose more by 1.2 years, and between 2000 and 2010 it rose by only one year. The data don't suggest that online dating is leading young people to linger in perpetual adolescence.

And, while online dating has boomed, divorce rates for young couples have actually declined. American couples who married in the era of e-dating were a bit *less* likely to divorce than couples who married before. Of women first married between 1990 and 1994, 25.5 percent broke up before their tenth anniversaries, compared to 28.9 percent of those married a decade earlier. Of women first married between 1995 and 2000, 10.5 percent failed to reach their fifth anniversaries, compared to 12.1 percent of those who had married a decade earlier.

These numbers do not in themselves refute Slater's argument, but they demand deeper analysis. Serious scholars have studied the effect of e-dating on commitment. The only one whom Slater quotes, psychologist Eli Finkel, says both in Slater's article and in his own writing about its consequences for commitment: maybe yes and maybe no; the effect isn't clear. Meanwhile sociologists Michael Rosenfeld and

Reuben Thomas have found that, other things being equal, couples who met online feel no differently toward one another than do couples who met in more traditional ways. Nor do those who met online have an elevated chance of breaking up after a year. Rosenfeld and Thomas did find that meeting in church or in grade school is probably the best way to ensure a lasting relationship.

Moreover, Rosenfeld and Thomas show that online dating can make a big difference for people who struggle to pair up in conventional circumstances:

> Young heterosexual adults [like "Jacob"] . . . are among the least likely to meet partners online. Young adults have single others all around them, which renders the Internet's search advantages mostly irrelevant. . . . The power of Internet search is especially important in identifying potential partners for individuals who face a thin dating market. Gays, lesbians, and middle-aged heterosexuals . . . are the groups most likely to rely on the Internet to find their partners.

The future that Slater fears—online dating *will* undermine commitment because it makes the alternatives to the person in front of you so plentiful and easy—may still come to pass. Or perhaps the opposite will happen: because online dating makes it easier for people to find the right match rather than a wrong match or no match, monogamy will be strengthened. Indeed, if there really are a lot of other fish in the sea, the competition may encourage partners to be especially good to one another, improving their relationships.

So far, there is little reason to be spooked that online connections are undermining personal commitment. But there may be a side effect worth noting. To the extent that online dating improves Americans' chances of meeting and mating the "right one" (and it does so especially for Americans past their twenties), it may accelerate a trend that started years earlier: American couples becoming more similar to one another in social class. Where once a lawyer married his secretary or a doctor his nurse, now lawyers and doctors marry one another; high school graduates are left with high school graduates. This growth in "marital homogamy" has contributed significantly to increasing economic inequality in the United States. Although rooted in women's entry into the workforce, especially into the professions, online matchmaking pushes that trend even further.

3. The Loneliness Scare

Headlines in *The New York Times* imply that if you're not feeling lonely, you may be the lonely exception: "Sad, Lonely World Discovered in Cyberspace"; "Alone in the Vast Wasteland"; and "The Lonely American Just Got a Bit Lonelier." Add books such as *Bowling Alone*, *The Lonely American*, and *Alone Together*, and you might think that there is an epidemic of loneliness.

An endemic epidemic, perhaps, because we have received such diagnoses for generations. The 1950s—the era of large families, crowded churches, and schmoozing suburbanites—brought us hand-wringing books such as *Man Alone: Alienation in Modern Society* and the best-selling *The Lonely Crowd*, which landed author David Reisman on the cover of *Time* magazine. About a half-century before that, policymakers were worrying about the loneliness of America's farmers, and observers were attributing a rising suicide rate to the loneliness of immigrants or to modernity in general. And so on, ever back in time. Noted historian Page Smith described colonial Americans' "cosmic loneliness" and the upset stomachs and alcoholism that resulted. Americans have either been getting lonelier since time immemorial or worrying about it since then.

The latter is more likely. Social scientists have more precisely tracked Americans' isolation and reports of loneliness over the last several decades. The real news, they have discovered, is that *there is no such epidemic*; there isn't even a meaningful trend.

If we turned to historians to measure Americans' degree of isolation over the centuries, they would probably find periods of growing and lessening social connection. The rough evidence indicates a general *decline* in isolation. When you think back to, say, a century ago, don't call up some nostalgic *Our Town* image (although alienation is a theme in that play). Picture more accurately the millions of immigrants and jobless, farm-less Americans trekking from one part of the country to another, out of touch with family and likely to be trekking again the next year.

Skeptical readers may vaguely recall an oft-repeated "factoid" that Americans have fewer close friends than ever. Sociologists at Duke reported, based on comparing two General Social Surveys, that the percentage of Americans who had no one to confide in tripled between 1985 and 2004, from about 8 to about 25 percent. Headlines ensued: "Social Isolation: Americans Have Fewer Close Confidantes" (NPR), "Social Isolation Growing in the U.S." (*Washington Post*). In 2009 the report's authors conceded, under pressure from a critic, that the valid estimate for 2004 isolation could be as low as 10 percent. (Disclosure: I was the critic.) Further research, published in the same academic journal in 2013, revealed that technical changes in the survey were responsible for creating the illusion that isolation had increased between the 1985 and 2004.

Several surveys conducted from 1970 through 2010 have asked Americans the same questions about their social bonds. The results, which I compiled in *Still Connected* (2011), show that some aspects of social involvement have changed since the 1970s. In particular, Americans these days sit down to fewer family dinners and host guests in their homes less often; eating and sociability continues, but outside the home. Americans communicate *more* frequently with their relatives and friends. Critically, Americans are *not* discernibly more isolated—but a few percent were isolated at any point in those decades—and Americans remain just as confident of the support family and friends provide.

Loneliness is different from isolation. People who report that they are lonely are not much likelier to be socially isolated than people who do not. But they are likely to lack one specific tie, to a spouse or partner. Roy Orbison knew that: "Only the lonely / Know the heartaches I've been through / Only the lonely / Know I cry and cry for you." Overall, Americans reported no more loneliness in the 2000s than they did in the 1970s. (In one series of polls, Americans reported the most loneliness right after the JFK assassination and again right after 9/11. Reporting loneliness may be a way some people report depression.)

Many commentators are sure that new technologies have made us lonelier. Literary critic William Deresiewicz wrote in 2009 about "the loneliness of our electronic caves . . . . The more people we know, the lonelier we get. . . . We have given our hearts to machines, and now we are turning into machines." In *The Atlantic*, novelist Stephen Marche blames Facebook: "We have never been more detached from one another, or lonelier. . . . We live in an accelerating contradiction: the more connected we become, the lonelier we are." (Remind me not to "friend" these guys; they sound so sad and overwrought.) MIT's Sherry Turkle, in *Alone Together*, reports on the torturous self-doubts that come with online friendship. Can she, her friends, and the young people she interviews really sustain intimate ties through their ubiquitous screens?

The first systematic studies of the Internet's social side suggested that early adopters were hiding away from people. But as Internet use became widespread, the findings changed. Robert Kraut, a leading researcher who had raised early warnings explicitly recanted; the resulting *Times* headline was, "Cyberspace Isn't So Lonely After All." People using the Internet, most studies show, increase the volume of their meaningful social contacts. E-communications do not generally replace in-person contact. True, serious introverts go online to avoid seeing people, but extroverts go online to see people more often. People use new media largely to enhance their existing relationships—say, by sending pictures to grandma. However, the 2012 report by Stanford sociologists Rosenfeld and Thomas whom I mentioned in the previous essay revealed that many more Americans are meeting life partners online. Finally, people tell researchers that electronic media have enriched their personal relationships.

People typically turn new technologies into devices for doing what they have always wanted to do. And people like to stay in touch. A century ago, Americans, especially women, turned two new technologies marketed for other purposes, the telephone and automobile, into "technologies of sociability." Similarly, developers of the Internet meant it to be a tool for the military and for scholars, and only a few imagined it might even serve business. Now users have made the Internet a largely social technology. (Not all new technologies develop this way; books and television are other, asocial stories.)

An intriguing exception to the recent handwringing is Eric Klinenberg's new book *Going Solo*. (Second disclosure: Klinenberg was a student of mine.) A far greater percentage of people now live alone than in the 1950s, and he interviews hundreds of them. However, most of them, Klinenberg stresses, choose to live alone. They'd rather pay more to do so than to live with kin or roommates. Many want a life partner but would rather live alone than with the wrong one. Klinenberg, like other researchers, finds that people who live alone lead, on average, as or more active social lives than do those who live with others. Single women, for example, spend more time with friends than married ones do. (In *Age of Innocence*, Ellen Olenska tells a puzzled visitor that she likes living alone "as long as my friends keep me from feeling lonely.")

Klinenberg is no Pollyanna. His 2003 bestseller, *Heat Wave*, revealed how old people living alone in dangerous neighborhoods died at high rates during the Chicago scorcher of 1995. They boarded themselves indoors and no one checked on them. And in *Going Solo*, Klinenberg also discusses living alone as a sad outcome rather than a happy option. Still, his overall story is that the great increase in living alone has not substantially increased loneliness. One reason, he suggests, is precisely the new communications technologies.

Loneliness is a social problem because lonely people suffer. But it's not a growing problem. Moreover, the loneliness that should worry us is not generated by a teen's Facebook humiliation, a globetrotter's sense of disorientation, or a novelist's romantic languor. It is, rather, the loneliness of the old man whose wife and best friends have died, the shunned schoolchild, the overburdened single mother, and the immigrant working the night shift to send money home. There's nothing new or headline-worthy about their loneliness, but it is real and important.

4. Is the Gender Revolution Over?

Nothing transformed American lives in the last century more than the gender revolution. The empowerment of women redefined courtship, sex, marriage, and child rearing. Women's entry into the paid workforce, in particular, upended the bourgeois Victorian family model in which "he" battles in the marketplace and "she" nurtures in the home. In 1950 about one in five married women went off to work; in 2000 about three in five did. Now, after decades of such astonishing change, the gender revolution appears over—before its completion.

In June 2012, Anne-Marie Slaughter, a former high-flyer in the State Department, wrote a declaration of dependence, "Why Women Can't Have it All," which stirred up blogo-pandemonium. She argued that the gender revolution will never be complete, because the emotional tug of family on women is too great, and the domestic urge of husbands is too slight. Then Marissa Mayer, the new head of Yahoo, returned to the office only two weeks after giving birth. "The baby's been way easier than everyone made it out to be," she proudly announced, signaling, to the outrage of struggling mothers that, for her at least, the revolution had already succeeded.

In early 2013, Facebook executive Sheryl Sandberg turned the Mayer moment into what she hoped would be a social movement. Her book *Lean In* argues that "[We women] hold ourselves back in ways both big and small, by lacking self-confidence, by not raising our hands, and by pulling back when we should be leaning in." Sandberg's Lean In Community provides confidence-building and hand-raising sessions for women. Critics charge that she is blaming women for their limited ascent in the corporate world when the problem is really sexism in the suites.

Critics also fault her for overvaluing careers themselves. In a *Dissent* essay former Facebooker Kate Losse attacked Sandberg on both fronts, explaining, "I decided to leave Facebook because I saw ahead of me . . . an unending race of pure ambition, where no amount of money or power is enough and work is forever. While I am not unambitious, this wasn't my ambition."

Anne-Marie Slaughter is not the first to declare that the gender revolution would fall short and that total victory might not even be worth winning. A front-page *New York Times* story from 1980—when Sheryl Sandberg was only eleven years old—reported on a survey of thousands of women attending elite colleges, with the takeaway that these late baby-boomers would delay or submerge careers for their children. For them the revolution was over, finished or not. Some "resented . . . pressures imposed by feminism: to work, to marry, to raise families without providing the answers to how all this should be done." A 1982 *Time* story on how professional women were stepping out to have babies quoted columnist Ellen Goodman: "You find women who have believed work is the end-all and be-all. But after eight years, they say, just like the housewives, 'Is this all there is?'" Feminist analysts worried that the revolution had stalled because employers—and male partners—had not yet really accommodated working women. Wives, in particular, faced what sociologist Arlie Hochschild in 1989 called the "second shift" of family duties at the end of a long workday.

Nonetheless, the revolution kept on rolling, through schools, offices, and our cultural assumptions. But not anymore.

I focus on young, college-graduate women, between the ages of 24 and 44, labeling them for brevity YCGW. Their enthusiasm for joining the workforce appears to have peaked in the 1990s.

Data from the Current Population Surveys, courtesy of the University of Minnesota's IPUMS Center, show a modest but real reversal in employment.

Around 1965, 67 percent of YCGW, today well into old age, were in the workforce. Around 1990, about 86 percent of them, largely baby boomers, worked for pay—a momentous nineteen-point increase. But around 2005, before the Great Recession hit, only 81 percent worked or looked for work, a drop of five points. In the mid-2000s, few of the non-workers among them said that they wanted a job—7 percent, down from 9 percent ten years before.

By the late 1960s, 54 percent of the married mothers among the YCGW were already in the labor force; that rate soared to about 75 percent in the mid-1990s. A decade later, however, the rate had slid to 72 percent. (By contrast, at least 98 percent of comparable fathers were in the labor force.)

But are we seeing a rebound, a turn again to work? Once the Great Recession hit, YCGW's labor force participation returned to levels of the mid-1990s. Circa 2010, as in the mid-'90s, 9 percent of those not in the labor force said that they wanted to be in it.

Which of the two trends—the post-'90s drop in work or the current rebound in work—augurs the future? Has the gender revolution been re-energized?

Birth rates suggest not. More college graduates are having babies, and they are having them earlier. According to Vital Statistics data, in 1995, 54 percent of first-time mothers with four or more years of college were over thirty years old, continuing a three-decade trend of delayed parenting. By 2002, however, the figure had dropped to 50 percent. Economists Qingyan Shang and Bruce A. Weinberg conducted a thorough analysis of childbearing through 2008 and found that college-graduate women in the 2000s had more children than comparable women did in the 1990s.

YCGW's attitudes about work also suggest that the gender revolution has peaked. In the 1970s, 98 percent of YCGW approved of married women earning money even if they had an employed husband. This fell to 91 percent in the 1990s. Other data point to little change in the last generation in YCGW's views on women at work.

In sum, the evidence on work, births, and opinions together suggests at least a leveling off, perhaps even a decline, in YCGW's commitment to work since the heyday of the late twentieth century. To what extent this shift resulted from changing attitudes among YCGW or from battle fatigue on the family-work front remains unclear.

Perhaps we have reached a new equilibrium. Given the constraints of our economy and social programs, given the norms of our culture, about 80 percent of highly educated young women, and 70 percent of the mothers among them, will work, give or take economic cycles. Maybe the great wave of social change has simply crested.

Or perhaps the Great Recession years foretell the future. More YCGW will work, as their less-educated sisters do now, because the new economy does not provide sufficient male employment. (Less-educated women did not work *any less* after the mid-'90s.) Americans will have to accept female breadwinners and maybe even male caretakers, although sociologist Philip Cohen has strongly rebutted the claim that the rise of women will soon make men economically dispensable.

Or perhaps once we are past the current crisis, YCGW will continue the swing back toward an older gender system. Returning to the '50s is hard to imagine, but the late '60s might not be. How could this happen? Many of the YCGW may look at their own second-shift mothers and declare that they will not make the same personal sacrifices. Many may decide that undoing the "motherhood penalty" in the workplace is too hard. Rising costs for informal childcare thanks to immigration reform and renewed economic growth may keep many YGCW at home.

Or perhaps one more big social policy push can bring full gender equality. Mothers in northern European countries work at rates about ten percentage points higher than American mothers do. However, they largely work at "feminine" part-time jobs because Scandinavian policies make it easy to work part-time and costly to stay home. American mothers mostly work full-time or not at all because part-time jobs here, sociologist Alex Janus suggests, have difficult hours, low pay, and negligible benefits. The Scandanavian model seems, despite great egalitarian efforts, to reinforce female-first caregiving.

Even if American YCGW are recalculating the work-family balance, the proportion opting out of the workplace is, so far, small. Moreover, other aspects of the gender revolution appear firmly fixed. For example, YCGW continue, in ever greater numbers, to endorse sexual freedom and women's political participation. But while highly successful mothers such as Slaughter and Sandberg carry on heated arguments about having it all, last century's greatest wave of social change does seem to be ebbing.

5. The Leisure Gap

SUMMER IN AMERICA: FOLKS SPRUCING UP RVs, parents packing kids' camp gear, airlines adding flights, and hotels raising prices. We know to expect much longer lines at the airports and traffic jams on the way to the beach. But what seems like a flood to us is a trickle compared to the tsunami of summer holidaymakers in Europe, as anyone who has been sardined into a European train, plane, or lane at the beginning of July and August knows.

Americans just don't vacation like other people do. Western European laws require at least ten and usually more than twenty days. And it's not just the slacker Mediterranean countries. The nose-to-the-grindstone Germans and Austrians require employers to grant at least twenty paid vacation days a year. In the United States, some of us don't get any vacation at all. Most American workers do get paid vacations from their bosses, but only twelve days on average, much less than the state-guaranteed European minimum. And even when they get vacation time, Americans often don't use it.

Perhaps Americans are Protestant-ethic work obsessives; we are likelier than Europeans to say that we want to work more hours than we do. But this leisure gap is a recent development. In the 1960s Americans and Europeans worked about the same number of hours. Leisure time then expanded everywhere— only more slowly and much less in the United States than elsewhere, leaving today's disparity. Some argue that high taxes in Europe discourage working, but economist Alberto Alesina and his colleagues point to legislation—that is, politics. The right to a long vacation is one of the benefits that unions and the left have in recent decades delivered to Western workers—except American ones.

Which brings us to the larger question. Just about everywhere in the West except the United States, where there is no mandatory paid time off, workers not only get vacations but also short work weeks, government health care, large pensions, high minimum wages, subsidized childcare, and so forth. Why is the United States the exception?

The answer comes in two general forms: one, Americans do not want such programs and perks because we do not want the kind of government that would legislate them. Two, Americans want them but cannot get them.

Of course, people usually want these benefits. So what's the problem? From one perspective, it's that those who cannot get them on their own—working-class Americans, generally—are not willing to band together and demand that government provide or require them. From another perspective, it's that the system does not let them do so.

Working-class Americans display relatively little of

the "class consciousness" that such solidarity requires. You can see it in the votes they cast and the answers they give in surveys. About one-third of those whom sociologists would consider working-class label themselves middle-class. Even though economic inequality is substantially greater in the United States than in Europe, Americans acknowledge less economic inequality in their society than Western Europeans do in theirs, and Americans are more likely to describe such inequality as fair, deserved, and necessary. Americans typically dismiss calls for the government to narrow economic differences or intrude in the market by, say, providing housing. Working-class voters in the United States are less likely than comparable voters elsewhere to vote for the left or even to vote at all.

Where does this unusual reluctance to think in class terms come from? Some on the intellectual left talk condescendingly about "false consciousness," the "What's the matter with Kansas?" complaint. But "false" is the wrong adjective. "Different" is better. American workers have not been brainwashed to love their masters; they are often independent, cynical, and subversive. (In the words of the song "Take This Job and Shove It," "Well that foreman, he's a regular dog, the line boss is a fool. . . .") They weigh considerations apart from class. One is the insistence on self-reliance, which weakens calls for class solidarity. Another is the set of moral concerns, such as "family values," that may trump personal economic interests. And they may calculate their economic interests in ways that just don't add up to some observers on the left.

Others point out that American class identity has always been trumped by racial identity. Plantation owners rallied poor southern whites to fight for slavery; factory owners recruited black scabs to break strikes in the north; the GOP developed a "southern strategy" to recruit white voters resentful of the Civil Rights agenda. American class exceptionalism is perhaps rooted in its slavery exceptionalism.

Yet others argue that American culture has simply been, and remains, too individualistic to allow the rise of either European-style class consciousness or the faith in big government that would allow for many of the kinds of programs that reformers have secured in other industrialized nations.

For one or more of these reasons, Americans don't vacation because they don't want the kind of leftist government that would legislate vacations.

The alternative answer to the vacation question is that working-class Americans *do* want the vacations—and the rest of the welfare state package—but are blocked by our political system.

The historical record is full of literal blockages. For example, state governors have often sent National Guard troops to shut down strikes and demonstrations. More broadly, features of American democracy itself may undercut working-class mobilization.

The first such feature to come to mind in the Super PAC era is money. Money mattered before *Citizens United* and it matters even more now. Legislators don't necessarily sell their votes, as many openly did decades ago, but campaigns run on the fuel of money.

Those with the most run the farthest.

How American democracy is built matters at least as much. For one, it's unusually hard for working-class people to vote here. From about the 1830s to the 1920s, political machines made voting easy: they shepherded laborers to the polls; rewarded them with liquid refreshments, music, jobs for relatives, and sometimes cash; handed out prepared party tickets to be cast in the ballot boxes; and deployed party symbols to aid the illiterate. Good-government progressives overturned that. They developed a civil service; instituted the secret ballot; required separate-day registration, citizenship, and literacy; promoted nonpartisan local elections; and generally raised the bar for voting. These reforms and others drove turnout down to the pitiful levels of our era. No wonder, then, that American policy decisions ignore the views of working-class voters almost entirely.

Also, American democracy is built for stasis. Power is dispersed to local arenas and local elites, typically with conservative consequences. Opponents of social change can man the system's many veto points, including the usually conservative Supreme Court. Even having a two-party system, as opposed to a multi-party one, seems to undermine working-class political influence.

The they-don't-want-it and they-can't-get-it views are not irreconcilable. In great measure, what people can imagine as possible, normal, or right depends on what they already have. Some of us can recall when the proposal to create Medicare was widely assailed as socialized medicine. Now few Americans can imagine a country in which the elderly go without taxpayer-provided health care. But the structural impediments to working-class action can then become impediments to working-class consciousness itself—which, in turn, makes action less likely. A tight circle of American exceptionalism.

Those who would intervene in that tight circle face a tough task, but a possible payoff. There have been breakthrough moments—the New Deal, the Great Society—when the political stars aligned. Part of the conservative resistance to Obamacare is the fear that, once running, it will come to be seen as an "entitlement," as a right. For opponents, this is a reasonable worry. People can get used to all sorts of new rights, which then become fixed in the political system—just as Europeans expect four weeks' vacation, no matter how crowded things get.

6. How to Be Poor

You're working a casual job, maybe in construction or at the gas station, paid a bit over the minimum wage with no benefits—one of those jobs that comes and goes. A buddy wakes you up with a desperate call: he needs a ride right now; you're the only one; at least your car runs. He lent you $200 last Christmas when you were scuffling; he's one of the old school crowd who party together and look out for each other. If you say yes, you will probably be late to work and might get fired. On the other hand, the boss is probably going to lay you off when things slow down in another month or two. What do you do?

We like to think that we are responsible for our own happiness and financial well-being. One way that idea has manifested itself is in the "culture of poverty" debates, which have recently made a comeback—only this time it's about whites. Charles Murray, of *The Bell Curve* fame, stirred up the argument anew when he dropped his latest look-how-outrageously-frank-I-can-be book, *Coming Apart: The State of White America, 1960–2010*, into the media hot tub. This time around, however, we understand much better why, when, and how culture affects poverty.

Murray's own cultural analysis is not serious. Working-class whites are trapped in the 1960s counter-culture of sex, drugs, and rock-n-roll, he says. While middle-class kids grew up, tossed away the love beads, and became solid citizens, the proles couldn't get untangled and are now raising—as single parents—a third generation of wastrels. Let's turn instead to the important issues.

That economic differences between less-educated and more-educated Americans have widened in the last four decades is no longer news. Neither is it news, at least to scholars, that gaps in lifestyle, such as marital status, child-rearing practices, and community involvement, have also widened. The classes have even grown more spatially apart. The controversy Murray unleashed concerns the role of culture in these differences; specifically, do the "white trash" bring misfortune on themselves by the bad values they hold and the bad choices they make?

To answer those questions, we might start with cultural analyses of poverty developed in the 1960s. Anthropologist Oscar Lewis reported that many Mexicans and Puerto Ricans were trapped in poverty in large part because they held and passed on to their children worldviews that hamstrung their efforts to advance. Daniel Patrick Moynihan adapted the notion in his unfairly castigated 1965 report describing the increase in black out-of-wedlock births. Analysts in the 1980s used the term "underclass" to mean roughly the same thing: the chronically poor are guided by a distinctive and debilitating culture of fatalism, suspicion, cynicism, thrill-seeking, and disregard for bourgeois morality.

Legions of social scientists bristled at these analyses because they seemed to "blame the victim." Lewis, Moynihan, and others had argued that the culture of poverty arises in the first instance from poverty, but that point was lost in popular and policy translation. The loud objections drove culture of poverty discussions out of fashion.

But fashion, as it often does, turned. In 2010 the *New York Times* reported, "'Culture of Poverty' Makes a Comeback," hooking the story on a just-published collection of professorial essays entitled *Reconsidering Culture and Poverty*. The 2010 argument is more nuanced than either the 1960s version or the media version, but still controversial.

Critically, understand that the long-term poor are a small minority of a minority. Most of those counted as poor in a given year are poor temporarily because of setbacks such as layoffs, family break-ups, car breakdowns, or medical emergencies. (Note, too, that we are not talking about the severely physically or mentally disabled; the controversy is about the able-bodied.) Social welfare scholar Mark Rank estimates that about half of all Americans will be poor sometime between the ages of 25 and 75, and perhaps a fifth will go through both poverty and affluence. Only about 2 percent, perhaps even less, will be poor most of their lives from 25 to 60 years of age.

These few able-bodied and chronically poor are explained, popularly, in either of two ways. One: they are just like us, but without money. They will drop whatever distinctive habits they may have, such as bearing children out of wedlock, once they are economically secure. Two: the long-term poor are different from us. Give them money or offer them a job and they will still breed out of wedlock—and get stoned, and fight, and oversleep. The poverty is in their heads and is therefore deserved.

Culture matters, today's scholars say, in part because it provides us with the values to which we aspire. But the chronically poor share middle-class values.

Researchers repeatedly find that poor unwed mothers wish for and usually expect to wed; they want a conventional family in a conventional house. Similarly, surveys show that students from poor families have high hopes and often high expectations for college. So the cultural issue is not purpose and values.

Culture really matters because it provides us with a cognitive "toolkit" (in sociologist Ann Swidler's phrase) of understandings, guidelines, and interpersonal skills that we use to pursue our values. Middle-class Americans, for example, generally act with self-confidence, demand their rights, follow regular schedules, trust others, and schmooze with the right people. Poor Americans typically know about these "strategies of action" but often have not mastered them or, crucially, have not found them useful in their worlds.

In their worlds, staying humble is usually the best way to keep their jobs or their kids in school. Sharing what money they have rather than saving it, or risking a job to drive a friend, increases the odds that they will be helped when the inevitable crisis hits. And where there are many predators, it makes sense to be distrustful or even predatory in turn.

Sociologist Martín Sánchez-Jankowski describes two sorts of lifestyles to deal with scarcity and insecurity. One is to hunker down, hoard what you have, and take no risks, because tomorrow is unpredictable. The other is to step out, spend what you have, and live for today, because tomorrow is unpredictable. Neither adaptation is a script for middle-class success, but a middle-class script would usually fail in conditions of insecure jobs, needy relatives, and chaotic neighborhoods. These adaptations allow the poor to make a life.

The culture debate now comes down to asking how much these adaptations become a force of their own. People find it hard to change habits, they teach their children to see the world as they do, and they are swayed by the views and practices of their neighbors. Thus, even if opportunities emerge, the chronically poor may fail to grasp them; they may be too fatalistic, too suspicious, too committed to local ties, too scared. People, in sum, learn life habits suited to conditions of scarcity, but those habits can keep them in those conditions. Where might we break that cycle?

The American impulse is to target the culture—teach abstinence, discipline kids, lecture parents, preach punctuality, provide moral training—so that the chronically poor will be ready when opportunity knocks. The alternative, more European, is to target the opportunity structure—provide jobs and practical training, guarantee health benefits and housing—so that tomorrow is more predictable and middle-class scripts are more practical.

Most social scientists, especially those who know "white trash" the best, would say that our chances of long-term success are much greater with the second approach. Habits are hard to change; absent an environment that rewards new habits, why take the risk? Since the mid-nineteenth century, most Americans adopted historically new industrial and bourgeois habits, not just because ministers, teachers, and settlement workers pushed those habits—although they did—but mainly because those habits worked in a new economy.

You are less likely to get that early-morning call for a ride if your buddies have secure incomes. But should one call and the job you could lose is itself secure and well paid, your calculations about how to respond will change—and so will the lessons you pass on to your children.

7. Extremely Local

Americans care about, prefer, and trust the local over the national. On the whole, we seem to believe our happiness and well-being depends on it. But we bear some serious consequences for this ideal.

A survey experiment reported in 2012 illustrates this preference: respondents who read a story about an American soldier killed in Afghanistan were more likely to turn against the war if he was identified as coming from the respondent's state. And in 1998 Tom W. Smith of the National Opinion Research Center collected surveys showing that on topics ranging from schools to violence to morality, Americans rated conditions in their localities better than in the country as a whole, sometimes by huge margins.

Local bias is well known in politics. Americans think Congress is terrible, but their own representatives aren't so bad. In early 2013, only 16 percent of Gallup respondents approved of how Congress was handling its job, but 46 percent approved of their own representatives' work. Americans want representatives to respond to local rather than national interests. Although evidence suggests that local governments are neither more honest nor more efficient than the federal government, Americans generally trust local pols more and believe that they waste less money than the feds do. Never mind that the number of federal employees essentially stopped growing nearly twenty years ago, while the number of local employees grew 16 percent between 1993 and the Great Recession. These contrasts have persisted or even strengthened in recent years.

There are several possible explanations for the seeming statistical oddity that Americans' average evaluation of the nation is far worse than the sum of their evaluations of their own neighborhoods. Perhaps people compare the personal experiences they have locally with sensationalist media coverage of the nation. Perhaps it's simply hometown boosterism. Or perhaps it's the result of a deep, historical commitment to the ideology of localism.

That Americans prefer neighborhood and community to distant authority is no big surprise. Right and left agree: "think globally, act locally." And these days "locavores" are all around us. But more important than slogans is how much and how distinctively localism is built into the American political system.

Compared to other nations, a startling proportion of American law and policy is determined by states, counties, cities, and smaller jurisdictions such as school districts and homeowner associations. These units determine most of our taxes—how much we pay, on what goods, according to what rules. Some New Yorkers, for instance, make a point of filling up their cars in New Jersey, where gas taxes are lower. Tax burdens also vary within states. A nice new car will cost me a few hundred dollars less in sales tax if I go up the road to buy it in Davis instead of in Berkeley. Even our urban areas are split into distinct municipal enclaves—for example, Beverly Hills surrounded by Los Angeles.

These local jurisdictions define justice—what are crimes, what are penalties—and policing. Compare laws and enforcement with regard to alcohol sales, pot smoking, or panhandling, or contrast police policies toward undocumented immigrants in, say, Phoenix and New Haven.

Small governments decide what our children will learn—how many schools will teach what subjects with what staffing in what languages. Shall we teach evolution, or testing skills, or creativity? And the money available to do whatever kind of teaching varies notably from district to district.

Localities have their own building codes and zoning laws. A municipal rule requiring large lots for houses is one way to ensure that only the affluent can buy into a town. Communities even have their own labor laws regarding credentials, wages, and benefits.

In 2014, the minimum wage in San Francisco was $10.74, $8.00 in Los Angeles, and $7.25 in Houston.

And the list goes on. I close with an obvious example: Since 1971, the Constitution has required that the age of voting everywhere be eighteen, but just about everything else that determines who can vote, when, and how is controlled by states and counties. Political struggles over voting laws are being fought district by district.

Other Western democracies have some features of localism (Switzerland is a noteworthy case), but the United States is extreme. Many comparable countries have national or regional, not local, police; a national judiciary; a national sales or value-added tax; a national program for training and assigning teachers; national labor laws and labor contracts; and so on.

American localism has persisted even though the role of the federal government has grown over our history. That expansion started in the nineteenth century, notably with the Lincoln administration's transcontinental railroad, land-grant colleges, and homesteading, among other initiatives. In the last century, the federal income tax and broad interpretation of the Constitution's commerce clause have given Washington the tools to deal with pressing issues of the modern world. The feds, for example, established old-age pensions and health care, built most of the major roadways, and established air quality standards. Washington sometimes coerces states and localities to do its bidding—for instance, by threatening highway funds to make states raise the drinking age. Nonetheless, and despite conservative outcries about violating the original intent of the Constitution's authors, these extensions are, by world standards, only modest modifications to American localism.

Arguments for America's exceptional localism, aside from fealty to the founding fathers, rest on democratic impulses and concern for practical management. We generally believe that the closer the governors are to the governed, the stronger the control the latter have over the former. Furthermore, we value people in each community determining their own way of life. Let Manhattan be Manhattan and let Provo be Provo. Such localism also allows individuals to choose from a "menu" of communities in search of the one that suits them best—low taxes with crowded schools versus high taxes with small classes, for example.

A political science argument for localism is that the states and localities are the "laboratories of democracy," that experimentation and competition among local units yields new and better ideas that can be adopted elsewhere or by the federal government itself.

Critiques of America's exceptional localism also rest on democratic impulses and concern for practical management. Practically, localism creates races to the bottom. Jurisdictions outbid each other to subsidize businesses that play one against the other for the best deal. In the end the "winning" locality often loses money on the deal. Localism also makes it harder to raise up depressed regions. The South, most notably, lagged far behind for much of American history. Breaches in localism such as the Works Progress

Administration (resisted by many Southerners), the Tennessee Valley Authority, and federal community aid helped the South catch up.

As to democracy, local authorities often enforce injustices against isolated people who can gain effective voice only by combining at the national level. The Civil Rights movement is a key example: national coalitions used federal power to break state and local Jim Crow systems. The Fourteenth Amendment has been used to impose national values over local resistance on behalf of individuals' free speech, religious liberty, and legal representation. American localism, moreover, can corrode democracy by encouraging people to shirk wider civic responsibilities. Advantaged Americans cloister their money, attention, and citizenship behind the boundaries of affluent suburbs or the gates of private communities, leaving the less advantaged to cope on their own.

These, then, are some of the trade-offs. We govern close to the grassroots, in accord with the localism that is a distinctive part of the American democratic experiment. But we pay a price for it, literally and morally.

Part II

Policy for a Happier America

8. The Good Life

Battles over social policy are fought in the trenches by hardened politicians. But scholars serve, too. They are the ammunition mules, providing the combatants with ideas, arguments, and evidence. Following the ghetto riots of the 1960s, Lyndon Johnson empaneled a committee of wise men who, in turn, retained many scholars to help the president defend Great Society programs against the anticipated backlash from "middle America." The Kerner Commission concluded on the basis of social science research that the uprisings were the product of poverty and white racism. Richard Nixon spoke up quickly for many in middle America when he charged that the report "blames everybody for the riots except the perpetrators." Johnson may have wished for a more nuanced report, but he did use it, as he later used the report of a commission on the history of violence in America, to protect his agenda for a larger, more beneficent welfare state. Of course, the backlash came nonetheless—spurred on by the pandemonium that was the 1968 Democratic Convention—and it sent the Great Society into retreat.

That backlash, ridden to power by Nixon and even twelve years later by Ronald Reagan, created a tactical opening for the free market battalions. For a couple of decades now, influential economists have successfully argued that wealth—and presumably human well-being—would be maximized by removing constraints on business: cut taxes, regulations, tariffs, food subsidies, and the like, and entrepreneurship will flourish. And so will we all. The marketeers' success in shaping policy here and abroad is clear. Clear, for example, in World Bank demands that governments of developing nations stop subsidizing their poor; in the elevation in our courts of a "Law and Economics" philosophy, which seems to consider the bottom line as important as the legal line; in campaigns for school voucher programs; and in a system of corporate regulation that maximizes shareholder returns above everything else, including jobs and community interests. Under such heavy assault, defenders of an activist and equalizing state, of FDR's and LBJ's visions, have resisted in part by drawing on social scientists to question the intellectual premises of this market invasion.

The free market, these scholars argue, is a fantasy. Market activities are deeply "embedded" in social relations. You can see that embeddedness writ large in the way government spending decisions and tax codes inevitably favor some investments, industries, and even specific businesses, over others. (The George W. Bush administration, cheerleader of the free market, was a case in point. Some may recall the ever-presence of the Halliburton company.) You can see embeddedness writ small in the way businesspeople prefer to deal with friends rather than cold-bloodedly pursuing the maximal deal. Even among commodities traders, the financial is personal. And you can see embeddedness in the many ways that market-driven spending is socially inefficient. Exhibit A: the American health care system. The United States is first in the world in per-capita health spending, twenty-fourth among OECD nations in life expectancy. Critics of market logic have also attacked the standard criterion for identifying success—maximizing wealth, especially as it is usually measured by Gross Domestic Product (GDP) per capita. Finally, no event more dramatically reveals how the social undergirds the economic than the vast credit bailout that the Bush administration proposed for Wall Street in September 2008 and the Obama administration pursued. (It was a bit like watching Toto pull the curtain back to reveal that the Great Oz was a creature of the professor.)

One breakthrough in the intellectual counterattack against the marketeer is the United Nations' Human Development Index (HDI), a measure of how well a nation is doing. The composers of the index specifically demoted wealth to only one of three equal indicators. The other two are life expectancy and education, as measured by adult literacy and school enrollment rates. Each of the three goals, advocates of the HDI argue, is equally important to quality of life. The political implication of the HDI is obvious: welfare-state initiatives, such as teacher training and mosquito abatement, matter as much as business expansion. Or, at minimum, business expansion is valued according to its positive effect on education and health. In the 2012 World Bank rankings, the United States was third among large nations in price-adjusted GDP per capita. In the same year's UN ranking of nations by HDI, the United States was third, behind Norway and Australia. However, the UN also presents "inequality-adjusted" HDI rankings that discount scores that are skewed; in that ranking, the United States comes in around fifteenth to twentieth.

The Measure of America: American Human Development Report, 2008–2009 opens the domestic front in the struggle over defining the common good.

Written, compiled, and edited by Sarah Burd-Sharps, Kristen Lewis, and Eduardo Borges Martin, funded by the Rockefeller Foundation and Oxfam America as well as other notable organizations, supplied with background papers by serious researchers, guided by a blue-ribbon advisory committee, and blessed by Nobel Prize–winning economist Amartya Sen, the book makes the case for adopting humane standards beyond wealth and argues for specific programs to meet those standards.

Measure sells its project in part by constructing an American version of the HDI and then offering rankings upon rankings of states and congressional districts by their overall American HDI and other statistical measures. As magazine publishers well know, rankings sell—the hundred greatest movies, twenty top cities to visit, forty most innovative colleges, whatever. Here you can find your state's or your congressional district's standing on dozens of dimensions, but most especially on HDI. The project's Web site has provided numbers updated to 2008 and there we find that Massachusetts Congressional District 8 (as drawn in 2002), where sat the offices of *Boston Review*, ranked sixty-ninth out of 434 in overall HDI. My Berkeley, California, CD 9 ranked thirty-fifth. But both languished far below the king of the mountain, New York CD 14, which included western Queens, Manhattan's Midtown, Central Park, East Side, and Turtle Bay. Turtle Bay is home—by coincidence?—to the United Nations. On the bottom rung was California CD 20, the largely rural Fresno area, home to many poor Mexican immigrants.

Measure's message, the compilers tell us, is that we need to replace an understanding of progress that asks "how is the economy doing?" with one that asks "how are people doing?" Then we will see that America is not doing well. It is slipping behind other countries. And it has great internal inequalities, especially along the lines of class and race. Redressing those inequalities, lifting the HDIs of places like California CD 20 and of the nation as a whole, will require major public investments.

Measure is thus that hybrid, the political scholarly document. Such hybrids inevitably contain tensions between the scholars' compulsion to describe the world in all its complexity and murkiness and the policy analysts' need to deliver unmuddied analyses and simple plans and to sell them boldly. Yet even before *Measure* is a book of scholarship and a political platform, it is a statement of values.

Measure assumes, as does the United Nations' HDI, that the good life in the United States is about three things: living long, going to school, and being wealthy. Many Americans would be dissatisfied with this definition and the results it yields. Most, I suspect, would not consider New York CD 14 the best place to live—even if they could regularly lunch at the Museum of Modern Art and even if they could afford to live there.

When they decide where to live, Americans certainly weigh a community's healthfulness, level of learning, and earning opportunities as important criteria. The latest American HDI index, from 2013, accordingly puts Connecticut, Massachusetts, and New Jersey the top of the state list. But Americans looking for new homes also give great weight to space—indoor space in bedrooms and rec rooms and the outdoor space of yards and access to nature. And they are, of course, constrained in their choices by housing affordability. The top two states for spaciousness and affordability, at the time of *Measure's* writing, were North Dakota and West Virginia (ranked twenty-sixth and fiftieth by the HDI). Americans also look for neighborhoods that are safe from violent crime. That put Vermont and Maine in the top few safe states in both the earlier and the most recent data (but only fifteenth and twenty-fifth in the latest HDI rankings).

Most Americans value family as central to the good life. All but a relatively few Americans, for example, prefer to be married. The two states that ranked highest in 2000 and a decade later in the percentage of people fifteen and older who were married were Idaho and Utah, but these states ranked only only forty-second and twenty-third in the latest HDI. These two states are also among the best to go to if you want to live where women generally do not have births out of wedlock. In one passage, the authors of *Measure* note that children thrive best when raised by two biological parents, yet that is not factored into their index. The back of the book lists several dozen social indicators, including relative availability of maternity leave, but not incidence of divorce, abortion, or out-of-wedlock births. The magazine *Best Life* had made its own rankings of the one hundred best cities to raise a family, drawing on measures that included school test scores, number of pediatricians, divorce rates, and commuting times. Their top three cities were Honolulu, Virginia Beach, and Billings, Montana (in the 76th-, 138th-, and 328th-ranked congressional districts by the author's HDI rankings).

For many, perhaps most, Americans, faith is also central to the good life. The states where people most often report going to church were, in 2010, Mississippi and Alabama, both ranked in the bottom five by HDI. You may value "community" in the sense of neighbors helping one another. Rates of volunteering in 2012 were highest in Utah and Minnesota, twenty-third and seventh in HDI. And, what about just attaining some peace of mind? Estimates suggest you will find fewer depressed people in South Dakota and Hawaii, which are thirty-first and tenth in the latest HDI scores.

Simply put, human development for one person may not be human development for another. *Measure*'s set of standards is a difficult sell to average citizens and the politicians whom they elect because it is grounded in the worldview of Manhattan's East Side or—to list the remaining top five congressional districts the book presents—of Virginia's eighth, Alexandria, and California's fourteenth, forty-eighth, and thirtieth: Silicon Valley, coastal Orange County, and western Los Angeles County (from Malibu to Santa Monica to Beverly Hills—human development 90210-style). What might grate the average American is not so much the final rankings—although no one likes to be assessed as mediocre—but the failure to acknowledge the question of whose values we should maximize. Then again, the average American may not be the audience for this book.

If we look at a couple of the HDI's more technical features, we can see there as well that decisions that seem merely procedural have significant implications. One would not know from the text of *Measure* that there is a sizeable statistical literature on the construction of the United Nations' HDI. Take the one-third of the HDI that represents wealth. The current international version of the index uses, mainly for lack of an alternative, a lousy number— per capita Gross National Income. (Per capita measures of wealth are lacking because they mask how equally or unequally wealth is distributed. A relative handful of Bill Gateses, Warren Buffets, and Oprahs makes average Americans look richer than they really are. Thus, the UN's new inequality-adjusted statistics.) *Measure* uses instead the median earnings of all workers aged sixteen or over. Much better, but still freighted with issues.

This indicator, for example, ignores the number of people who are unemployed. So the District of Columbia could easily rank first in the income component of the book's HDI even though it had the fifth-highest unemployment rate (and second-highest poverty rate) in the nation. Furthermore, both the earnings and the unemployment statistics ignore people who are incarcerated. Given that the District ranks highest in crime rates, it probably also ranks high in young men behind bars. In addition the earnings measure lumps together part-time and full-time workers, which means that communities where many teens work after school—middle-class neighborhoods—consequently do not look as rich as they really are. As a last example of technical pitfalls, the compilers of *Measure* do not adjust earnings for cost of living. What would happen to the HDI scores of Manhattan's East Side or Los Angeles' West Side if one dared include the rent?

These formulas, numbers, and rankings seem

largely for show. Some of the book's assertions have no support in the back pages, and the authors often state as fact claims that, while certainly plausible, remain hotly debated in the research literature—for example, that investing in schools significantly improves cognitive development, that firearm availability causes homicides, or that the quality of neighborhoods substantially shapes the quality of children. And yet, *Measure* is good enough for government work: despite its myriad flaws, its conclusions are sound and sensible enough to guide policy. New policies cannot await the certainties that scientists demand of one another. The United States is clearly underachieving in its commitment to provide its citizens with life, liberty, and the opportunity to pursue happiness. We are an exceptionally unequal society, and in many ways that inequality is widening. (As one example, the money provided for college assistance has been shifting from lower-income to higher-income families just as borrowing for college has become an acute problem.) American inequality injures not only those on the short end but also the nation as a whole. We have much to learn and to copy from other nations. To stay with the status quo is itself a policy choice, one premised on claims about society that are far less substantiated and defensible than those in this book.

This brings us to reading *Measure* as a political document, which it is meant to be, complete with Web site, Capitol Hill briefings, and mission statement:

> to stimulate fact-based public debate about and political attention to human development issues in the United States and to empower people to hold elected officials accountable for progress on issues we all care about: health, education and income.

Godspeed. I assume that the phrase "issues we all care about" is intended to suggest that these are goals everyone can subscribe to, unlike, say, gay rights or environmentalism. But if *Measure* means to convert the unconverted, it does not try very hard. Not only does it not directly address the question of whose values we measure, but the kind of progress the compilers seek is defined by an obviously liberal wish list: universal health insurance, supportive housing for the homeless, compassionate care for the elderly, gun control, two years of universal preschool, widening the scope of standardized tests, and so on. They do not give serious consideration to the personal-responsibility agenda of activists on the other side, much less to small-government or personal-freedom agendas. Barack Obama lectures black parents to read to their children, but *Measure* proposes sending registered nurses into homes to teach parents how to parent and recommends paying mothers to take their children in for check-ups. Moreover, the authors barely address the price tag for their policies, how to pay for them, cost-benefit analyses, or what the order of priority ought to be.

Do these concerns indict any effort at applying statistical measures to our understanding of the good life? Of course not. Scholars have made great progress in measuring, for example, wealth, economic inequality, upward mobility, academic achievement, crime, and even faith and psychological well-being. Serious public policy discussions need to incorporate such data. What social scientists cannot provide is the final weighting and summing up of all the values we hope to maximize, the single yardstick, the rankings of "best" to "worst." That is the duty of citizens and their elected officials.

As a political-scholarly hybrid, *Measure* is not likely to persuade people on the conservative—or even the moderate—side of current debates. The scholar's fantasy of politics as a courtroom where experts present the researched facts and a learned public adjudicates wisely rarely becomes reality. Yet, *Measure* arms progressives with more arguments, evidence, data, and numbers—many, many numbers—to challenge the worldview that adding dollars to the GDP is a sufficient public agenda. Other analyses do so as well and are perhaps less vulnerable to criticism. For example, Howard Steven Friedman's 2012 book, *The*

Measure of a Nation, offers a simpler presentation that compares the United States to other western nations on a variety of key indicators and argues that the results suggest we have much to learn from our western peers. There is also, of course, a large academic industry in comparative sociology. Such studies are enlightening but typically find few readers.

In the larger scheme, the political struggle of ideas and research is dominated by the media, which floods public debate with so-called "experts," and by think tanks that present multi-color brochures to Washington staffers at well-appointed conferences. In that way, money speaks louder than scholarship in shaping our sense of the good life.

9. Accidental Billionaire

"It's not about you," declares Reverend Rick Warren, the celebrity minister and hair-blown invocationer of Barack Obama's first inauguration, in his bestseller *The Purpose-Driven Life*. It's about God's purpose for you. Malcolm Gladwell's *Outliers* and Gar Alperovitz and Lew Daly's *Unjust Deserts* also declare that "it's not about you." For that matter, it's also not about Bill Gates, Warren Buffett, Beyoncé, Gordie Howe, or any other wildly successful individual; it's about the circumstances you and they were lucky enough to fall into.

Both of these books argue that a person's success depends more on being born in the right place and at the right time than on being the right person.

"Success," concludes Gladwell, "follows a predictable course. It is not the brightest who succeed. . . . Nor is success simply the sum of the decisions and efforts we make on our own behalf. It is, rather, a gift." This is a difficult message for Americans to understand, raised as we are in a culture that insists more than any other that every individual earns and therefore deserves his or her own fate.

Whether Gladwell and Alperovitz and Daly can change the way Americans think about success is another matter. The authors have a strong wind at their backs: the Great Recession displaced so many workers and depleted so many savers' accounts through no obvious faults of their own that it becomes harder and harder to believe that everyone is getting their just deserts.

In *Unjust Deserts*, Alperovitz and Daly attack the moral claim that the wealthy have earned—and therefore deserve—their wealth. The key observation they insist and elaborate upon is that most of everyone's wealth today comes from the efforts of earlier generations, particularly their contributions to knowledge and technology. Even Bill Gates's rise to fortune depended on the development of electricity, the know-how to fabricate plastics, the invention of wireless communications, the silicon chip, and all the other technologies that Microsoft products presume, not to mention the markets, schools, law, and other institutions that make any large, modern business possible. Most of the difference—almost all of it, probably—between the way Bill Gates lives in 2014 and the way his ancestors lived in 1814 was determined before Bill was even born. In the last two centuries, the per-capita wealth of Americans increased twenty-fold. He and we simply inherited almost all of that increase.

Therefore, Alperovitz and Daly argue, neither Bill Gates nor we earned most of our wealth; and thus neither Bill Gates nor we *deserve* most of our wealth. Cumulative knowledge is "the overwhelming source of all modern wealth [and] comes to us today through no effort of our own. It is the generous and unearned gift of the past."

If this is so, then most of what we have, and especially most of what the wealthy have, is, in economists' terms, unearned "rent." It is income we pocket without having produced it, like the landowner whose property multiplies in value once the state builds a highway nearby. As John Stuart Mill put it, "that increase of wealth which now flows into the coffers of private persons *from the mere progress of society*" is not morally assignable to that person (emphasis in *Unjust Deserts*).

Who, then, should profit from the increase in wealth that the past has gifted us? Alperovitz and Daly answer: society, which provided that wealth. "Society—all of its members equally—must be the residual claimants to the inherited contributions of past generations; . . . These contributions are of sufficient magnitude to warrant significant social claims on private wealth." And thus the authors conclude, we have moral warrant for significant income redistribution.

This is the heart of what the authors call the "knowledge inheritance" argument for equality. Alperovitz and Daly also address topics around that argument. They point out, for example, that new inventions themselves are also largely gifts of the past. Breakthroughs come not from individual strokes of genius, but as the predictable fruit of expanding, collective knowledge. If it had not been Einstein, it would have been someone else pretty soon, because the scientific community had teed up his stroke. They challenge the conservative think-tank canard that more equality of outcomes impairs economic growth. It quite clearly does not: several statistical studies show that there is no meaningful correlation between changes in equality and changes in growth rates. One case in point is post-war America, where an economic boom accompanied decreased wealth disparity. Alperovitz and Daly also review the philosophical arguments over what justifies differences in wealth.

Even though *Unjust Deserts* has a clear political

commitment, it is well-reasoned, well-documented, well-argued. I am convinced. But would skeptics be?

There are at least a couple of seams in the argument. One is the repeated assertion that the wealthy have "siphoned off" the bounty from "inherited knowledge." That is not obvious. Over several generations, the poorest in our society have gained on the richest. Differences in life spans have narrowed considerably, as have differences in access to basic goods. Although this equalizing trend stalled in the last generation, history suggests that the "knowledge inheritance" may already have been redistributed—at least somewhat—toward equality.

Another seam opens in the authors' claim that society should redistribute the unearned rent from the past equally to all. Perhaps it should not be distributed at all, but invested in common goods, like a cleaner environment. Or perhaps it should be distributed in accord with how much each individual today makes of and adds to the commons. Those who best harvest the past and plant for the future should, some could reasonably claim, be richer than others.

The authors note this last objection to their case for redistribution, but too briefly. They answer it mainly by shifting the debate to new grounds: since opportunities in modern America are not equal, they say, those who succeed have not really deserved their greater reward. This move takes us into the terrain of Gladwell's *Outliers*.

Malcolm Gladwell, the fantastically successful *New Yorker* journalist, best-selling author, and lecture-circuit star, also has a message of humility: "It is impossible for . . . any outlier," any highly successful individual, including himself,

> to look down from their [*sic*] lofty perch and say with truthfulness, 'I did this, all by myself.' . . . They are the product of history and community, of opportunity and legacy. Their success is not exceptional or mysterious. It is grounded in a web of advantages and inheritances, some deserved, some not, some earned, some just plain lucky.

CLAUDE S. FISCHER   95

Gladwell parses the luck of the outliers into three categories: accidents of birthdate, accidents of cultural heritage, and just plain accidents.

The first lesson Gladwell delivers is that luck explains at least part of success. To a startling degree, the year and month someone was born predicts how well he or she will do. Sports provides some clear evidence. It is the arena of achievement in which native talent should most determine who gets ahead. Yet, month of birth is critical. Would-be athletes born just after the cut-off dates for youth sports leagues are much likelier to end up, years later, as successful players and even professionals than those born near the end of the twelve-month period.

Several processes explain this "relative age effect." The child who is among the older in a league—say, seven years and eleven months old on opening day of the seven-year-olds' baseball season—will typically be bigger, more mature, and more experienced than the child who is seven years and three months old on opening day. The older will have more success, enjoy the sport more, get more attention from coaches, and be more likely to make the all-star team. Each year the process repeats and the advantages feed on themselves, so that by, say, fifteen, the traveling teams are composed of players whose birthdays bunch up at the early part of the league calendar. One's success is, then, partly an accident of how one's birthday matches league rules.

(This example strikes home. My quite athletic daughter had the misfortune of being born ten days before term, in late December instead of early January. Consequently, she was regularly the youngest in her leagues, instead of the oldest. With better luck, she could have gone much farther. Many parents understand this dynamic and hold back their children in school to maximize sports success.) Gladwell's book has reinvigorated research and debate on the relative age effect across many domains. In hockey, at least, it appears that by the time players reach elite levels, later-born ones often shine—but only because these especially talented men have managed to overcome systematic calendar discrimination to make it to the top.

Accidents of the calendar can affect more than athletic achievement. They also figure in academics. A child's age relative to the starting date for school is worth—other things being equal—several percentile ranks on achievement tests. The relative age effect lasts, probably compounds, over time and substantially influences students' chances of going to college.

Year of birth matters even more. Geeky teens who ended up as high-tech moguls seem to have been born in the mid-1950s, and many major American industrialists of the nineteenth century were born in the 1830s. The reason for the birth clusters, Gladwell argues, is that new economic opportunities emerged in a concentrated moment, just when those men reached maturity.

Gladwell may be cherry-picking his examples, but more systematic data also show that "cohort effects" can be powerful. For example, men born a decade or two before the Civil War grew up shorter and died earlier than men born before or after those years. Women born earlier in the twentieth century were expected to interrupt their careers for the duration of their children's school years, but women born later were not. Americans who entered old age after the 1970s were half as likely to be poor than those who entered old age before the 1970s. How much money a college degree could earn you fluctuated sharply in the 1970s and '80s. And Baby Boomers seem particularly vulnerable to depression and suicide.

We are living through another demonstration of cohort effects. Many students who left high school, college, or graduate school in the Great Recession started their careers later or on a lower rung than their older siblings did and than their younger siblings will probably do. The classes of '09 through perhaps '13 did nothing to "deserve" the economic handicap they will carry through life. Such is the fickle hand of fate.

The other fateful accident Gladwell dwells on is of a different nature: the fortune of being born into the right culture. Drawing on superb scholars as varied as historian David Hackett Fischer, sociologist Annette Lareau, and psychologist Richard Nisbett, Gladwell argues that families inherit and pass on distinctive habits. Those habits may be rooted in the exigencies of life centuries earlier—herding in the borderlands of Britain, toiling in the rice paddies of southern China—but, according to this controversial theory, they influence descendants to this day. To be born in the American South or to Chinese-American parents is to inherit the habits, respectively, of reacting violently to any implied insult and of persisting intensively in the face of any problem. The former culture raises the child's chances of failure in life, the latter of success.

Cultural inheritances are not fixed, Gladwell reassures readers. People can be retrained—as the successful Knowledge Is Power Program does when it conditions students to persist. And, other research shows, people can adapt their strategies to shifting circumstances. But culture of birth, like timing of birth, is one those accidents that partly explains success.

Gladwell compares the biographies of Christopher Langan and Robert Oppenheimer. Both were identified as geniuses in childhood, and both demonstrated their ability early in life. But Langan ended up a college dropout, semi-recluse, and unknown because, Gladwell argues, his parents never taught him—as Oppenheimer's had taught their son—critical social skills. Oppenheimer could get his college to help him find therapy after he tried to poison his teacher, but Lanagan could not get his college to overlook some late paperwork.

Finally, there are just plain accidents. Tech giant Bill Joy, formerly of Sun Microsystems, had the blind luck of choosing to attend the University of Michigan. When the programming bug hit him in his freshman year, he found himself—by the happiest of accidents—in one of the few places in the world where, thanks to the university's pioneering of computer time-sharing, a seventeen-year-old could program all he wanted. High-powered attorney Joe Flom was also "lucky" when, in 1947, the white-shoe law firms he applied to after law school rejected him because of his "antecedents," that is, being Jewish. Forced to go out on his own and accept whatever business walked in the door, Flom was in the right place when takeover entrepreneurs who needed legal work came along.

Gladwell tells stories about extreme successes, about "outliers," but he means to convey a broader message. He aims to demonstrate "that extraordinary achievement is less about talent than it is about opportunity." He concludes that the "patchwork of lucky breaks and arbitrary advantages that today determine [*sic*] success" ought to be replaced "with a society that provides opportunity to all." By such comments, Gladwell opens the door to a vast, long-lasting and complex research arena that he barely acknowledges.

For at least five decades, social scientists have used enormous surveys and complex statistical tools precisely in an effort to explain "status attainment." How much, they ask, of the variation in people's life outcomes—who gets ahead and who falls behind—can be explained by individual traits and how much by circumstances? In 1972 Christopher Jencks and his colleagues published one milestone study, *Inequality*, which emphasized opportunity but also concluded that much variation cannot be explained and so must be due to "luck." In 1994 Richard Herrnstein and Charles Murray notoriously stirred the waters with their book *The Bell Curve*, which argued that individual success or failure was largely determined by a person's basic intelligence, which in turn was determined by his or her DNA. Gladwell notes neither book, although he is surely aware of both. (In 2007 Gladwell had to recant a reference to *The Bell Curve* that included the word "notoriously"; I shan't.)

Scholars have waged the person-versus-circumstances argument with regression coefficients, simultaneous equations, hierarchical linear modeling, monozygotic versus dizygotic twin studies, and other apparatuses of modern social science. One provisional conclusion is that Gladwell's summation, "achievement is less about talent than it is about opportunity," remains unresolved. (For example, many psychologists now assert that the sort of social skills that advantaged Oppenheimer over Lanagan are themselves the product of genetic coding.) I stand on Gladwell's side in this debate, but we probably cannot yet say what portion of success is the result of native ability; circumstances like timing of birth, family advantages, and teacher quality; and dumb luck.

Even as the empirical issue remains fuzzy, so does the deeper philosophical one. How do we decide what is individual talent and what is luck? Take the child who works intensively at school and ends up with a Harvard M.D. We might attribute the child's work habits to, say, the hard push that Jewish-American parents or, more recently, Chinese-American parents provided (the so-called "tiger mom" pattern). Gladwell calls that child "lucky" for culturally inheriting a strong work ethic from his or her parents— being in the right womb in the right decade. Others might call that child "motivated"—"what difference does it make whether the child's motivation was culturally or genetically inherited?" they could ask—and assert that that now-grown child is deserving of both success and the sense of pride it provides.

Alperovitz and Daly suggest a thought experiment: where would the Bill Gateses of today be if they were transferred to the "state of nature"? How much good would their technical or business skills do them there? Absent society, their skills would gain them little. Therefore, the wealth of the real Gateses is not really their own accomplishment. Gladwell is not as radical while making his claims for equalization, but the implications of *Outliers* are similar.

This may, however, be the wrong thought experiment. Perhaps we need to think the way baseball statistics nerds do, applying the thought experiment of VORP: value over replacement player. The basic idea—never mind the complications—is that a player's worth is measured by what he contributes to winning compared to what the next available replacement for him would contribute. This roughly captures the marginal value of the player. If we think that the next available head of Microsoft after Gates (or, for Apple fans, of Apple after Steve Jobs) would have contributed less total value to global productivity, then Gates deserves credit for a healthy chunk, perhaps all, of that difference. This thinking leads to a contrary conclusion, then, about inequality. It is the sort of argument boards of directors make in justifying huge CEO salaries: that the difference between the best and next-best candidate is worth millions.

Perhaps there is another line of argument about desert, which is not about trying to assess justice by proportional reward, but trying to assess justice by a compassionate moral yardstick. We do not feed children or care for the elderly—or for "the least of these"—in proportion to their value over replacement, but in response to their humanity.

Both the social science and the philosophy of *Unjust Deserts* and *Outliers* can be parsed and trimmed. But they surely help puncture the egoism of the successful and remind them that "it's not about you."

10. Mind the Gap

THE STRONG VERSION OF RICHARD WILKINSON and Kate Pickett's argument in *The Spirit Level* implies that President Obama's fight to reform health care was pointless. Extending the availability of health insurance cannot substantially improve Americans' health. Instead, the president would make us all happier, healthier, and longer-lived, their logic suggests, if he could get the richest, say, 5 percent of Americans to leave the country.

Wilkinson and Pickett, eminent health scholars from the United Kingdom, present considerable evidence correlating unequal incomes in nations or American states with negative outcomes in physical health, mental balance, levels of violence, social integration, teen births, school performance, and seemingly everything else. Inequality, they explain, makes people focus on status and their relative positions on the prestige ladder. Such obsessions, in turn, create anxiety, distrust, and social isolation, which raise people's level of physiological stress. Finally, stress, as we all now know, exacts high costs. It weakens the immune system, for example, and drives people to poor coping behavior such as overeating and lashing out at others. Through these steps, *The Spirit Level* argues, economic inequality becomes bad for everyone's health.

But does this psychological explanation really account for the harms of inequality? And just how sure are we that the social ills Wilkinson and Pickett canvass are even caused by inequality? Whether we accept their psychological framework determines to some extent how we will respond to problems of inequality, and in hewing to it, the authors generate some pretty tepid solutions.

Measuring inequality

The Spirit Level does *not* argue simply that being poor is bad for people. Indeed, in developed societies, the authors insist, an individual's wealth is not critical. It is of course healthier to be rich than poor, but what matters most for Westerners are the *gaps* between the rich and the middling and the poor in their societies. Wilkinson and Pickett reject economic growth as a public-health policy, in part because such growth might benefit the affluent as much or more than those of lesser income. Income differences would not necessarily shrink, and it is these gaps that we must mind.

For proof, the authors present dozens of similar, paired graphs. Across the bottom of each graph is a scale running left to right from low to high income inequality. On the vertical axis is a measure of the prevalence or intensity of a social problem, such as obesity or depression. The authors plot the locations of several Western countries and Japan, and the dots typically line up such that the more inequality, the worse the problem. In the international comparisons,

CLAUDE S. FISCHER   111

Japan almost always falls in the bottom left corner of the space—low inequality, few problems—while the top right of the space—high inequality, many problems—mostly is reserved for the United States. In the U.S.-focused versions of these graphs, states take the place of nations. The states do not line up quite as neatly, but the pictures convey the same message: more inequality, more bad stuff.

One of this book's virtues is how straightforward and reader-friendly its prose and figures are. Wilkinson and Pickett also crisply and lucidly summarize research drawn from nearly 400 scholarly references. The authors anticipate criticisms, take pains to explain complex issues, and respect the reader. And as someone who many years ago coauthored a book on the hazards of inequality, I am sympathetic to their project. But are their numbers right? Is there an association between inequality and bad outcomes—do the graphs tell the whole truth? And, if there is a correlation, is inequality really the major cause of all those problems?

One concern is how we measure inequality. Researchers often use a measure of the distribution of income—usually, the "Gini coefficient"—or compare the income of the richest 10 or 20 percent of the population to that of the poorest 10 or 20 percent. In recent years, we have become sensitized, for example, by books such as Piketty's *Capital in the Twenty-First Century*, to the fact that a big chunk of our growing inequality involves the richest one-tenth of one percent pulling away from everybody else.

Different metrics produce different results. Good and comprehensive measures of inequalities in accumulated *wealth* rather than annual income show much greater inequality: in 1999 an American family at the 80th percentile of income made about two times what a family at the 50th percentile did, but the family at the 80th percentile in wealth owned about *six* times the assets of the 50th-percentile family. On the other hand, good and comprehensive measures of *consumption* indicate less inequality: a family at the 80th percentile of spending paid only 1.5 times as much for food and clothing as did a family at the 50th percentile. American families almost all the way down to the very poorest own cars, televisions, and the like, and some commentators point to such consumption numbers to dismiss the concern about income inequality.

Using a metric other than money also changes the picture. For instance, while inequality in how much people earn has widened considerably in the United States for about four decades, inequality in how long people live has narrowed somewhat.

A second question about the empirical basis for the connection between inequality and well-being is whether the authors have fairly examined all the bad outcomes. A major omission in their graphs is the suicide rate, which is considerably *lower* in more unequal countries. The authors try unpersuasively to explain this correlation away, contending that in unequal societies people project their status anxiety outward, blame others rather than themselves, and thus end up killing others rather than themselves.

Another outcome Wilkinson and Pickett ignore is the rate of births to unwed mothers, which also trends *downward* as inequality rises, especially if one brackets anomalous Japan. (By the way, anyone can easily play this game of chart-your-bad-outcomes by ransacking the Web sites of the U.S. Census Bureau, the Organization for Economic Co-operation and Development, and the U.N. Human Development Report—source of the HDI index discussed in the previous essay—and then copying the tables into spreadsheets.) The authors may have overreached by implying that virtually every social ill can be blamed on inequality.

Finally, there is the problem of what the aggregate numbers mean for any given person. Wilkinson and Pickett's graphs are displays of what are called *ecological correlations*, that is, they represent the connection between the income inequality of a country (or state) and some *average* outcome—say, average life span, or average risk of being obese. Such averages hide huge variations within countries and states, variations that overlap. The average Japanese man will live four years longer than the average American man, but many millions of American men will outlive many millions of Japanese men. Ecological correlations based on averages vastly overstate the actual connection between inequality and *individuals'* life spans. This is not just a technical quibble. A substantive implication of this distinction is that it is better for your health to be rich in America than to be poor in Japan, no matter what the average differences between the two nations are.

Wilkinson and Pickett would respond that it is still healthier for both the rich and for the poor to live in Japan than in the United States. Whether that is so gets yet more complicated. But even if the graphs exaggerate the implications of national inequality for individuals, we can allow the authors this: in a Rawlsian sense, if you did not know how rich you would be, then choosing to be born in a more equal society would, all else staying constant, decrease your risks of many bad outcomes. How much of a decrease is difficult to estimate.

Sven versus Jack

Grant that inequality is often correlated with bad outcomes. Is inequality therefore the cause? With overly bold claims such as, "we have shown that reducing inequality leads to a very much better society," Wilkinson and Pickett assert that there is more than a correlation here, that inequality is a—perhaps the primary—cause of bad outcomes such as violence, short lives, repression of women, psychological depression, and so on. Here is where most of the academic controversy focuses: is there some other factor that is really at work, such that income inequality is just a side issue? Researchers have put much of the data Wilkinson and Pickett use onto statistical torture racks trying to extract truthful confessions, but they often elicit only garbled croaks.

Some critics argue that these ecological correlations between inequality and average outcomes are just a statistical illusion arising from the fact that the health benefits of each additional dollar are greatest for people of low incomes and marginal for people of high incomes.

Others hold that some X factor, perhaps as yet unidentified, explains *The Spirit Level*'s graphs. My own candidate, which I invite others to test, is cultural—the *Sven versus Jack factor*. If you look at most of the book's graphs of nations, you will see that the "good" quadrant—low rates of inequality, low rates of problems—is largely composed of Nordic and northern European nations (and non-Western Japan, which should be bracketed). The "bad" quadrant is largely composed of the United Kingdom and its former colonies. Continental European nations fall into a mushy middle. If you look at most of the U.S. state graphs, you generally see in the good quadrant northern tier states, such as Minnesota, which were heavily settled by descendants of Scandinavia, and see in the bad quadrant southern states, which were much more intensively settled by highlanders from the British Isles. Thus, the Sven versus Jack factor.

The Nordic-British contrast also corresponds to

the difference between social democratic and neoliberal states, an elided distinction that only further confuses cause and effect. Is there something about the Nordic region's history or culture that leads those nations to be welfare states, relatively equal, and healthy, and something about Anglo-Saxon history or culture that does the opposite—with varying levels of inequality simply a byproduct?

Wilkinson and Pickett understand these sorts of objections and have responses, both technical and logical. One strategy for handling the correlation-is-not-causation issue is to look at historical change: in cases where inequality has dramatically risen or fallen, what consequences followed? Unfortunately, here one starts cherry-picking examples. When East Germans were integrated into the rest of Germany, they joined a more economically unequal society, and their young people got more obese. Score one against inequality. On the other hand, between 1970 and 2005, income inequality in the United States, as measured by the Gini index, grew about 20 percent, but homicide rates *dropped* 30 percent. More systematic studies of what follows from changes in inequality tend to be more equivocal.

Researchers have not sorted out the causal issue yet, but the best provisional judgment is probably that economic inequality contributes something, albeit much less than the authors claim, to some health and social problems, but, again, fewer than the authors claim. Even the skeptics, however, do not argue that inequality is good for anyone except those on the top of the pyramid.

Psychology, politics, and solutions

If inequality does, to some degree, cause social problems, why? Wilkinson and Pickett emphasize that the mechanism here is social-psychological: inequality creates anxiety about status and feelings of unfairness that eat at people. In the words of a chapter title, "inequality gets under the skin." Unlike the volume of studies on the correlation between inequality and health, there is little research that directly tests this proposition. The authors collect a variety of suggestive evidence, such as laboratory studies on how people react to being put in low-status positions and primate studies on what happens when rankings among apes are messed with. But a lot of the case is built by argumentation and inferential stretch.

One recurrent issue in trying to explain any causal factor concerns the geographical level at which inequality operates. In the research literature, the strong correlations between inequality and bad outcomes tend to be seen when comparing nations, but when researchers compare smaller units, towns or neighborhoods, the connection between inequality at the local level and outcomes is considerably weaker. This is puzzling for the psychological analysis: wouldn't people be more psychologically affected by their neighbors' wealth than by the wealth of folks far away, say, in Malibu or on the Vineyard? The authors firmly argue that, no, what matters is where you—*and* your neighbors—fit in the national hierarchy; people know their national rank, and that is what generates the angst. Perhaps.

Even if people who feel they are at the bottom pay a psychological and health price for being down, are they not balanced out by those at the top who gain psychologically from being up? (In spite of the authors' claims to contrary, wealthier people are, according to available metrics, happier.) Shouldn't these two reactions balance each other out nationally? Wilkinson and Pickett would insist, in response, that everyone suffers psychologically from inequality, those at the bottom but *also* those at the top. In a status-riven society, the winners fear that their perches are insecure, and they know that there is a long way to fall. Besides, there's always someone to envy on a yet higher branch.

Is this psychological mechanism, a feeling of relative deprivation, necessary to explain the bad outcomes of inequality? One alternative, which the authors reject, is that it's really all about material disadvantages, not psychological angst. Wilkinson and Pickett say "no," and point to statistical studies suggesting that international variations in average income make less difference to outcomes than do international variations in the inequality of incomes. But the results are not all consistent. The authors also point to examples: low-income Americans are richer than low-income people in other societies, but Americans' health is worse.

A different explanation, suggested and documented by many scholars, invokes politics. They find that more heterogeneous societies and states— those highly divided by race, religion, and language, especially when accompanied by wealth differences— under-produce "public goods" such as community health care, safety, and education. For example, the higher the proportion of African Americans in a state, other things held constant, the lower the public welfare expenditures in that state. People in diverse nations or states may have greater trouble building the trust necessary for public action. Or perhaps the reason is that majorities in diverse nations or states resist spending their tax money on "those people."

Income inequality, then, may produce bad outcomes because class divisions in a nation or state lead to political paralysis or to unconcern by the wealthy about the fate of the less well-off. If the politics of inequality account for poorer health, then one might focus on politics as the route to fixing the problems. But Wilkinson and Pickett do not.

Their discussion of solutions dwells mostly on promoting employee-owned businesses, an odd focus. Such enterprises pay their executives less than typical corporations do, and Wilkinson and Pickett believe that their workers therefore have lower status concerns and less stress. Such workers may be more sympathetic to economic redistribution. But there is no logical reason why such businesses would beggar their neighbors any less than other businesses do, and this program hardly seems sufficiently muscular to bring American inequality down to Finland's level.

As I pointed out above, if the authors took their analysis literally, they might suggest direct manipulations of inequality: send the richest people—or, probably more efficiently, the poorest people—out of the country or the state. Inequality would go down and well-being would go up. Alternatively, leave the inequalities as they are, but devise ways to hide them from people—censor the media, say (no more tabloids profiling the lifestyles of the rich and famous)—so that people do not know their relative positions. That should, according to *The Spirit Level*, bring down crime, disease, obesity, and so forth. The authors do not go in these directions, and these are, of course, not plausible solutions in a democratic society. But they are the logical implications of *The Spirit Level*'s explanation.

There are more productive avenues they might have considered. The authors eschew economic growth to lift the poor because their data suggest that national wealth is not as critical as national inequality in affecting health, because growth might preserve or even expand inequality, and because growth violates their green principles. Further economic development in developed nations, they assert, is an exhausted route to greater well-being. Most economists, I am sure, would disagree. Most politicians, I suspect, would consider the dismissal of economic growth a wrong-headed strategy for electoral victory.

Similarly, Wilkinson and Pickett pay little attention to Robin Hood–like redistribution, which would attack inequality more directly (although not as directly as exiling the rich). Maybe they consider that program too obvious to expound upon, or perhaps too politically difficult to attain, or too tied into the very status concerns and materialism that explain why inequality gets "under the skin."

And there is little, if any, consideration in *The Spirit Level* for another strategy, one that tackles the specific difficulties of heterogeneous societies straight on: providing public goods in lieu of directly reducing inequality. National health insurance is one such public good; universal pre-school is another. The public, universal provision of water and sewer systems about a century ago did more than any other program to extend Americans' life spans in the last several generations. Proponents argue that such universal entitlements—Social Security and Medicare being the major examples—evade Americans' resistance to "handouts" and to explicit "leveling," and therefore have the highest chances of political success.

Given *The Spirit Level*'s overreach, it might seem easy to discount it. But Wilkinson and Pickett make a valuable contribution in enthusiasm and evidence, both of which will help fuel any effort to squeeze down the widening inequalities of our era. Realistically, that would require heavy political lifting in channeling economic growth more equitably.

European aristocrats traveling in nineteenth-century America were shocked at the status equality they found, and it expanded dramatically in the generations that followed. It helped create a society that provided enough security for average citizens to pursue their own happiness. Now, in the last generation and a half, that progress has stalled and, in many quarters, reversed. What is most alarming is not so much the psychological discouragement of seeing the top one percent soar so high, though that is certainly a crucial part of the story, but the new, seemingly insurmountable barriers that undermine material security. Those near the bottom fall farther behind, not just financially, but socially; for them, components of the good life—education, stable careers, marriage, and successful parenthood—have become harder to achieve and sustain. Those in the middle do better, but often at the cost of having to strive harder—juggling jobs and longer hours and few to no vacations), and mothers working who would rather not. Politics, perhaps once tilted to the populist desires of the masses, increasingly tilts toward reinforcing inequality.

But this tale may seem dismal only because we are still living in the wake of the Great Recession. Trends toward inequality and insecurity started earlier, around the 1970s. By some analyses, the current crisis is the "new normal"—or perhaps the broadening of the middle class in the twentieth century was the "old abnormal." Still, the wider sweep of American history suggests that the wheel can turn again, and that the equalizing, democratizing impulse to widen the pursuit of happiness can be reinvigorated. It is tempting to see America's 250-year sweep as one of straightforward progress, on the one hand, or a miserable decline from a Golden Age, on the other. But we should resist the temptation to adopt one of these easy narratives. Our collective pursuit of shared security has always been messy and inconsistent, but in the fray we have made progress. Messy inconsistency probably lies ahead, as well, as we continue the long American project of lurching toward happiness.

ACKNOWLEDGMENTS

The idea for *Lurching Toward Happiness*, adapted from essays I wrote for *Boston Review*, came from *BR* editor Deborah Chasman. She and Assistant Editor Matt Lord did most of the work, curating and editing the essays. Managing Editor Simon Waxman excellently edited most of the original essays that appeared in the pages of *BR*. I am also grateful to the excellent team at MIT Press. They all have my deep appreciation.

ABOUT THE AUTHOR

Claude S. Fischer is Professor of Sociology at the University of California, Berkeley, where he has taught since 1972. He is author of *Made in America: A Social History of American Culture and Character* and, most recently, *Still Connected: Family and Friends in America Since 1970*. He founded and edited *Contexts*, a general interest magazine of the American Sociological Association, and blogs at madeinamericathebook.wordpress.com. In 2011 he was elected to the American Academy of Arts and Sciences.

BOSTON REVIEW BOOKS

Boston Review Books is an imprint of *Boston Review*, a bimonthly magazine of ideas. The book series, like the magazine, covers a lot of ground. But a few premises tie it all together: that democracy depends on public discussion; that sometimes understanding means going deep; that vast inequalities are unjust; and that human imagination breaks free from neat political categories. Visit bostonreview.net for more information.